ENDANGERED AND EXTINCT ANIMALS OF THE RIVERS, LAKES AND WETLANDS

Michael Bright

FRANKLIN WATTS
London · Sydney

© Aladdin Books Ltd 2002

Produced by:
Aladdin Books Ltd
28 Percy Street
London W1P 0LD

ISBN 0–7496–4463–X

*First published in Great Britain
in 2002 by:*
Franklin Watts
96 Leonard Street
London EC2A 4XD

Editor:
Kathy Gemmell

Designers:
Flick, Book Design and Graphics
Simon Morse

Illustrators:
Tim Bramfitt, Barry Croucher
(Wildlife Art), James Field (SGA),
Mick Loates, Terry Riley,
Rob Shone, Stephen Sweet,
Mike Unwin, Ross Watton (SGA),
Maurice Wilson
Cartoons: Jo Moore

Printed in UAE
All rights reserved

A CIP catalogue record for
this book is available from
the British Library.

Contents

Introduction

Rivers, lakes and wetlands are fragile habitats and the animals living in them are exposed to constant change. A river can be in flood one day and a mere trickle the next. A lake or wetland can dry up and not reappear for months or even years. When people pollute the water or upset its normal cycle, the plants and animals that have adapted to the natural changes in water level are wiped out. As rivers are dammed, lakes poisoned and wetlands drained, the wildlife that depends on bodies of fresh water for its survival is in serious trouble. Many species have already disappeared.

Q: Why watch out for these boxes?

A: For answers to the animal questions you always wanted to ask.

zoom in on...

Bits and pieces

These boxes take a closer look at issues or the features of certain animals.

Awesome facts

Watch out for these dodo diamonds to learn more about the weird and wonderful facts on endangered and extinct animals and their world.

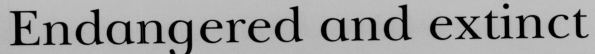

Endangered and extinct

When few animals of a particular species survive in the wild, the species is said to be endangered. If a species disappears altogether, it is extinct. Some extinctions are caused by human activities. Others are caused by natural events, like changes in climate or sea level, or competition from similar animals.

SYMBOL DEFINITIONS

In this book, the red cross symbol shows an animal that is already extinct. The yellow exclamation shows an animal that is endangered. Animals that are less endangered are said to be 'vulnerable'. Those that are more endangered and close to extinction are said to be 'critically endangered'. The green tick shows an animal that has either been saved from the brink of extinction or has recently been discovered. Many of these 'success' stories, however, are still endangered species.

Schomburgk's deer

Asian three-striped turtle

Whooping crane

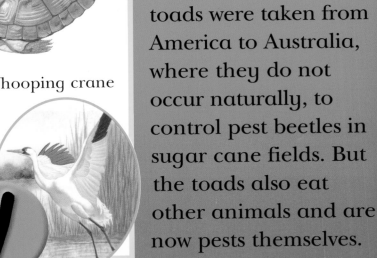

Animals that have been introduced into a particular habitat, accidentally or on purpose, are called alien animals. Cane toads were taken from America to Australia, where they do not occur naturally, to control pest beetles in sugar cane fields. But the toads also eat other animals and are now pests themselves.

Q: Does it matter if some animals become extinct?

A: Yes. Every plant and animal on Earth is important. Each has its role to play in the natural order. Removing one upsets the order and affects other living things. The overall picture of life on Earth – the variety of plants and animals, their behaviour and the ways in which they interact – is called biodiversity. Maintaining biodiversity is essential for the survival of all species.

The preservation of an animal's living space is critical for its survival. If its habitat is destroyed, it has nowhere to live and nothing to eat. Wetland habitats particularly are under pressure from the spread of industry and agriculture. The wild Asian water buffalo, which lives in wetlands, is now an endangered species.

For many years, people hunted wild animals without reducing numbers substantially. They killed what they needed to survive and did not take too much too often. With the widespread use of guns, however, people started to catch or kill too many animals, either for food or for fun. The once plentiful Bengali pink-headed duck was hunted to extinction in just a few decades.

River dolphins

River dolphins are primitive dolphins that live mainly in the fresh water of tropical rivers. They have a long snout, lined with many teeth, and very poor eyesight. Unlike marine dolphins, they have a flexible neck. River dolphins are threatened by pollution, hunting and dam building.

Yangtze river dolphin

The Amazon river dolphin, or boto, lives in the Amazon and Orinoco rivers in South America. It is said to catch fish alongside local fishermen, with one helping the other. But it is also killed for its eyes, which are sold as lucky charms.

!

! Fewer than 100 Yangtze river dolphins, or baiji, survive today. They are threatened by extensive dam-building projects on the River Yangtze in China. Some also get tangled in fishermen's nets or are killed in collisions with boats.

Awesome facts

About 100 Ganges river dolphins, or susu, are killed every year. Their oil is used to make catfish bait, even though bait made with fish oils produces better catches.

zoom in on...

Echolocation

To find their way, river dolphins send out sound signals and listen for the echoes that bounce back from objects in their path. This is called echolocation. Oddly, river dolphins can locate small fish in this way, but cannot 'see' the fishing nets in which they get caught.

Primitive fish

Some of the world's most ancient species of fish – sturgeons and paddlefish – are the survivors of an ancient group that swam in seas and rivers over 100 million years ago. But during the past 50 years, their numbers have declined drastically due to overfishing and pollution.

Freshwater sawfish

The Chinese paddlefish is one of the oldest living freshwater fish, but it is now a critically endangered species. Just 300 are left in the River Yangtze, where the population has dropped by 80 per cent because of overfishing.

!

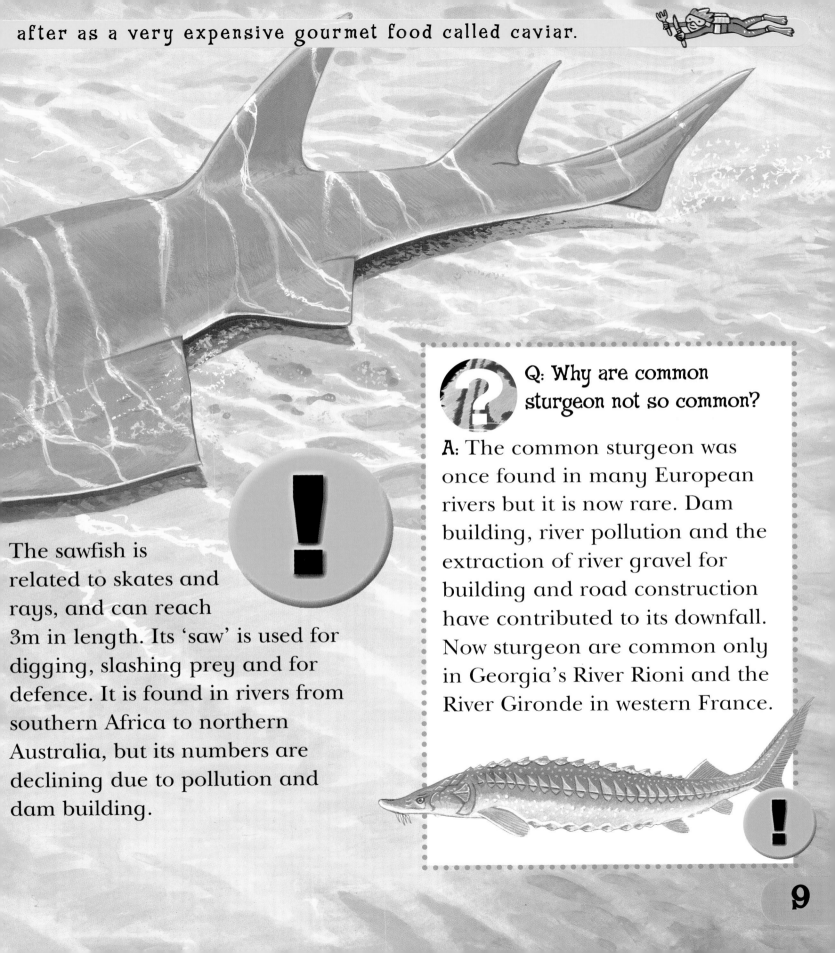

The sawfish is related to skates and rays, and can reach 3m in length. Its 'saw' is used for digging, slashing prey and for defence. It is found in rivers from southern Africa to northern Australia, but its numbers are declining due to pollution and dam building.

Q: Why are common sturgeon not so common?

A: The common sturgeon was once found in many European rivers but it is now rare. Dam building, river pollution and the extraction of river gravel for building and road construction have contributed to its downfall. Now sturgeon are common only in Georgia's River Rioni and the River Gironde in western France.

Huge shoals of New Zealand grayling once swam upstream from the sea, but the species is now extinct. It was gradually ousted from its native rivers when it faced competition from brown and rainbow trout. These were introduced so that settlers could go trout fishing. The grayling has not been seen since 1923.

Awesome facts

The rare Devil's Hole pupfish in Nevada is protected by law. Water can only be pumped from the lake if enough is left for the pupfish to survive and breed.

While farmed common carp thrive in European ponds, lakes and rivers, the truly wild carp of eastern Europe and western Asia is critically endangered. The wild population is expected to drop by 80 per cent over the next 10 years, due to pollution and introduced fish diseases.

Lost fish

Many species of freshwater fish have disappeared in recent years, but not all extinctions are due to human interference. The sculpin of Utah Lake, USA, was a casualty of the 1930s droughts. It died out when its traditional spawning grounds dried up as water levels dropped.

zoom in on...

Hot fish

The Tecopa pupfish swam in a hot spring in California, in the hottest water recorded for any fish. It was not discovered until 1942, but competition from introduced mosquito fish and pollution from a bathhouse ensured its extinction by 1960.

New Zealand grayling

11

Madagascar fish eagle

There are fewer than 25 pairs of wild Madagascar fish eagles left, making it one of the world's rarest birds of prey. Its numbers declined because its habitat had been disturbed. Nest sites are hard to find and the lake fish on which it depends have been overfished.

!

Fish eaters

Small fish are eaten by big fish, which are eaten by birds such as fish eagles. If pollutants enter this food chain, the poisons are concentrated at each link, until the birds at the top of the chain die. In this way, pesticides washed into rivers brought several bird species to the edge of extinction.

!

There used to be thousands of flightless Junín grebes at Lago de Junín, a high-altitude lake in the Andes, in Peru. Now only 50 survive. Their breeding lake has been poisoned by iron oxide waste from local quarries. The remaining birds may be moved to a safer place, but a suitable lake has yet to be found.

them against a branch.

The Ryukyu kingfisher is only known from a single specimen that was discovered on Miyako Island in Japan in 1887. It has not been seen since. It differs from related kingfishers in that it has red feet.

Ryukyu kingfisher

Awesome facts
Confused with a more common flying species, the flightless Atitlan grebe, from Guatemala, was discovered in 1862, rediscovered in 1929 and declared extinct by 1991.

The Bonin Islands in the northwest Pacific Ocean were isolated from people until a whaling ship was wrecked on Peel Island in 1826. Survivors set up a colony. Cats and rats escaped and all four native bird species, including the Bonin night heron, disappeared. The last bird was seen on nearby Nakondo Shima Island in 1879.

Bonin night heron

The critically endangered crested ibis of China nests and roosts in pine forests and feeds in rice paddies. Many were shot or fell victim to pesticides. One breeding population of 22 survives in the Qinling Mountains of southern Shaanxi.

zoom in on...

Dam building

Dam building can alter seasonal water levels and put the wintering sites of water birds at risk. The building of the Three Gorges Dam in the Yangtze Valley will disturb oriental storks and also upset the lives of Yangtze river dolphins.

About 2,500 oriental storks breed in eastern Siberia in summer and spend the winter in the wetlands of the lower Yangtze Valley and Hong Kong. Loss of trees to nest in, drainage of wetlands, human disturbance, hunting and pollution have all added to the decline of the species.

The bird is a long-distance migrant, so it needs to be protected over the whole of its range.

Herons and storks

Herons, storks and their relatives have long legs and stabbing bills. Many species live on wetlands, where they catch amphibians and fish for food. But many wetlands are being drained for agriculture, and pollution of rivers and lakes means that birds are losing their homes and their food.

Salt marsh habitats to the north and south of San Francisco Bay in California are home to the salt marsh harvest mouse. It survives there by being able to drink salt water. Its habitat is shrinking, however, because the wetlands are being drained for industrial and urban development.

Salt marsh harvest mouse

The endangered otter civet is not a good swimmer. It escapes from hunting dogs by running up trees, and ambushes fish and amphibians by waiting at the water surface with its eyes and nostrils exposed, like a crocodile. It lives in wetlands in Malaysia, Thailand, Sumatra and Borneo, but silt from mines, pesticides and other pollution are damaging its habitat.

!

!

Awesome facts
The giant river otter really is a giant. A large individual can be up to 2.5m long and is well able to tackle shoals of fish, such as catfish.

The Brazilian giant river otter is found in family groups in slow-moving rivers and ox-bow lakes alongside the Amazon River. It feeds mainly on fish. It is hunted illegally for its thick, brown, velvety fur.

River mammals

Rivers and streams provide a rich habitat for mammals, and many species take advantage of them. Fish and small shelled creatures provide food. It is easier to dig breeding burrows in soft riverbanks, and the water itself can be a safe place to hide from predators.

 Q: How does pollution affect river mammals?

A: Pesticides washed from farmland and waste from factories and mines can seep into wetlands. If they enter the food chain, they can poison wetland animals. Silt from mines and soil washed from deforested areas gradually fill wetlands and turn them into dry land.

17

Swamp deer

Several species of deer have adopted wetland areas as their home, including the marsh deer of Brazil and the swamp deer of India and Nepal. They feed on grasses or shoots. Hunting and the drainage of wetlands for agriculture are the main reasons for their decline.

zoom in on...

Antler medicine

Animal body parts feature strongly in oriental medicine, and deer antlers are no exception. Known as *nokyoung* in Korea, deer antler is prescribed to people who have problems with the liver and spleen. Children with growth disorders drink antler tea.

Kuhl's deer (left) is just 70cm high and lives in marshes and swamps on Indonesia's Bawean Island in the Java Sea. It is endangered by hunting and by the loss of its natural forests to make way for new plantations.

Schomburgk's deer was discovered in the swamps of Thailand in 1862, but few people ever saw it in the wild. It was killed for meat, and its antlers were used in oriental medicine. When its marshland habitat was drained, it moved to bamboo forests, but these were soon replaced by rice paddies and the deer were shot as pests. A policeman shot the last Schomburgk's deer in 1932.

Awesome facts

A test in New Zealand showed that deer antler velvet tonic, taken with a popular muscle-building supplement, can greatly improve athletes' muscle endurance.

Buffalo and hogs

Asian water buffalo are less aggressive than their African relatives, but the lesser water buffalo, or tamarau, is dangerous. Its home, Mindoro in the Philippines, was once uninhabited due to a virulent strain of malaria, but people now live there and the buffalo's habitat has been destroyed.

Awesome factS

Water buffalo have the largest horns of any cattle. The record was a bull shot in 1955 with horns measuring 4.24m from tip to tip along the outside curve.

The wild water buffalo is the world's largest buffalo. It lives in wetlands, where it cakes itself in mud to keep away bloodsucking insects. It once ranged from India, to Vietnam and Malaysia, but has been displaced by agriculture and is now restricted to India, Nepal, Bhutan and Thailand.

!

20

The lowland anoa is a miniature water buffalo confined to the swamp forests of Sulawesi, in Indonesia. It lives in small family groups, but little is known of its behaviour in the wild. It is considered endangered because it is hunted for its meat, hide and horns, and the marshes in which it lives are slowly being drained.

Agriculture

All wetland animals are threatened by their habitats being modified for agriculture, including flood control projects, forestry and livestock grazing. The pygmy hog – a small wild pig that lives close to rivers – now survives in reserves in Assam, in north India.

zoom in on...

21

The beautiful Bengali pink-headed duck from northern India is now extinct. It lived in grasslands, floodplains and small lakes and laid perfectly spherical eggs. It was common in the 1880s, and was usually caught as an ornamental bird, not for food. The introduction of shotguns changed all that, and the last wild individual was shot in 1935. Captive ducks survived in Foxwarren Park in Britain until 1942, when the last bird died.

Ducks

Ducks have been a target for hunters' guns for centuries, but the killing of most species has been regulated to ensure they are not overhunted. However, uncontrolled shooting still goes on in some parts of the world.

Fewer than 2,500 white-winged wood ducks are thought to survive in Asia. In Assam, they are known as 'spirit ducks' because of their haunting call. They are thought to breed in tree hollows.

zoom in on...

The Madagascar pochard is a critically endangered freshwater diving duck restricted to Lake Alaotra. Although one was seen in 1991, most have been killed by uncontrolled hunting. Parts of the lake have been converted to rice growing and a decline in water quality has made the duck's situation worse.

Egg thieves

Rats arrived on New Zealand's Auckland Island in 1839, when sealing and whaling stations were established. Along with introduced cats and dogs, the rats raided local Auckland Island merganser nests, on the ground and in tree hollows. By 1910, the mergansers were extinct.

23

zoom in on...

Dangerous journey

Waders are world travellers. Many species migrate long distances to and from wintering grounds in warmer lands. These are either in the southern hemisphere or in summer breeding sites on the tundra (northern plains). They fly in and out of the airspace of many countries, each with different conservation laws. A wader may be safe in one country and shot in the next. For endangered species, this may mean the difference between survival and extinction.

Waders

Waders are shore birds. They include plovers, oystercatchers, lapwings, avocets, sandpipers and many more. Most have long legs with which they wade in mud or in shallow water, and many have specialised bills for prising out food from the mud.

When a Tahitian white-winged sandpiper was approached, it ran off through the grass and then whistled as it took off. It was a ground-nester, so was vulnerable to rats brought by sailing ships. It was recorded in 1779 on Captain Cook's last voyage, but never seen again.

Just 60 black stilts are left in New Zealand. They nest on gravel banks in river channels. Introduced cats and ferrets have raided nests, and flood control programmes have destroyed nesting areas. Today, they survive in one valley on the Waitaki River.

Absent amphibians

Frogs, toads and newts have been disappearing at an alarming rate. Between 1960 and 1990, amphibian numbers dropped by 15 per cent worldwide and they continue to fall every year. Many amphibians have now gone altogether.

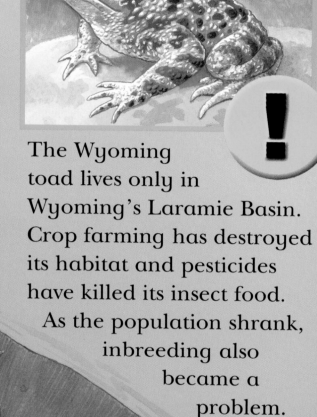

The Wyoming toad lives only in Wyoming's Laramie Basin. Crop farming has destroyed its habitat and pesticides have killed its insect food. As the population shrank, inbreeding also became a problem.

Golden toads live in the Monteverde cloud forests of Costa Rica. They are tiny creatures only seen when gathering at traditional courtship pools, but they have not been seen since 1987.

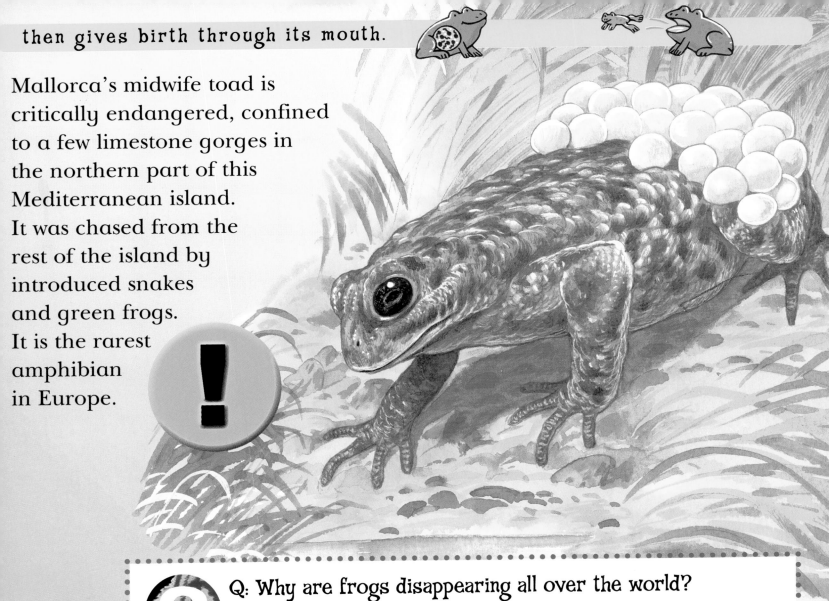

Mallorca's midwife toad is critically endangered, confined to a few limestone gorges in the northern part of this Mediterranean island. It was chased from the rest of the island by introduced snakes and green frogs. It is the rarest amphibian in Europe.

Q: Why are frogs disappearing all over the world?

A: Frogs' disappearance may be caused by global warming or pollution, or a virulent disease. A fungus called chytrid that destroys their skin, preventing them from breathing and absorbing water, has hit many species in Australia. Frogs also get red leg disease, which attacks their immune system.

The gharial of the River Ganges is a very long-snouted crocodile. Its numbers dropped to an all-time low in the 1970s, with only 300 left in the wild. A breeding and release programme in India has been successful and 3,000 now survive.

Gharial

Survivors from the age of dinosaurs

Dinosaurs were reptiles that disappeared 65 million years ago. Some of their relatives – crocodiles, turtles, snakes and lizards – survive to this day, but many of these are now threatened with extinction.

28

zoom in on...

Crocodile skin

Reptiles have a thick, hard skin that makes excellent leather. Crocodile and snakeskin are especially sought after for shoes and handbags. Several crocodile species, including the endangered Chinese alligator and several species of South American caiman, have been overhunted for their skins. Some are now reared in crocodile farms.

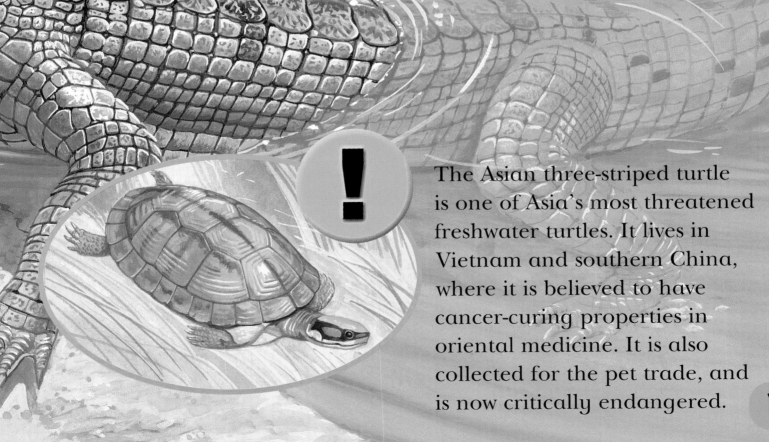

The Asian three-striped turtle is one of Asia's most threatened freshwater turtles. It lives in Vietnam and southern China, where it is believed to have cancer-curing properties in oriental medicine. It is also collected for the pet trade, and is now critically endangered.

29

Back from the dead

A good way to save species from extinction is to take wild individuals into captivity. Small groups are dispersed at different breeding centres to ensure that any outbreak of disease does not wipe out the entire captive group. The young of the successful breeding groups can then be released back into the wild.

 Q: Who decides when an animal is endangered?

A: The IUCN (International Union for the Conservation of Nature and Natural Resources) co-ordinates research about surviving plant and animal families. The status of each species is assessed and the findings are published in Red Data Books. The buying, selling, hunting and poaching of wild animals is monitored by CITES (Convention on International Trade in Endangered Species of Wild Fauna and Flora).

In 1937, there were just two small breeding populations of whooping cranes in North America. Due to conservation efforts, there are more than 300 birds today. Small, captive-bred flocks have been released at sites where the birds were formerly found.

Glossary

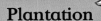

Amphibian
A backboned animal that lives both in water and on land, such as a frog.

Drainage
The removal of water from land to prevent waterlogging or to create drier land.

Endangered
Describes a species which is likely to die out if the factors causing its decline continue.

Extinct
Describes a species not seen in the wild for 50 years.

Food chain
The transfer of food and energy from plants through a series of animals that eat then are themselves eaten.

Habitat
The place where an animal lives, usually characterised by the plants that grow there.

Inbreeding
Breeding with closely related individuals, which often results in weak breeding stock and diseased young.

Introduced
Describes a species brought by humans into a habitat where it does not occur naturally.

Mammal
A backboned animal with hair, such as a cat or a human, which feeds its young on milk.

Migration
The movement of animals to and from their winter feeding grounds and their summer breeding and feeding grounds.

Oriental medicine
A form of medicine from the Far East that uses parts of plants and animals to help prevent or cure diseases.

Overfishing
The catching of too many fish, which may cause a fish population to disappear.

Pesticide
A chemical used to kill plants and animals considered pests.

Plantation
An area of trees or other plants that are planted by people in order to harvest their wood, leaves or fruits.

Pollution
Damage caused to an area by chemical or biological materials such as oil, sewage and industrial wastes.

Population
A group of individuals of the same type.

Predator
An animal that hunts and eats other animals.

Range
The area in which an animal lives for most of its life, including places it visits often.

Reptile
A backboned animal with scales that lays eggs, such as a crocodile.

Species
A group of animals that resemble each other and are able to breed together.

Index